www.johnweiler.co

If you are interested in the author's writing services, please contact him via the website.

The Website Homepage Blueprint

Write a homepage that wows prospects, proves your credibility and converts visitors to clients using a proven, step-by-step formula

To my parents,

who to this day continue to offer encouragement in my career and life.

TABLE OF CONTENTS

Introduction

What does your homepage say about your business?

You want a homepage that converts.

One that impresses prospects, proves your credibility and highlights your value.

But you're a bit unsure how to do that.

What does a credible, impressive homepage look like? How long should it be? Where do you talk about your business's story, product benefits and services?

You probably have many questions. And you may feel overwhelmed when you sit at your computer and view or think about your homepage. Homepages are critical to converting visitors to clients after all.

They're the most visited page on any website and oftentimes your first impression online. What's more, if you write a boring, confusing or awkward homepage, visitors will bounce. In other words, there's money and business on the line—so there's a lot at stake.

But don't worry.

This book is here to help.

As it says in the title, it's literally your homepage blueprint and I promise it will demystify and simplify how to create your homepage.

Why listen to me?

I have worked in digital marketing since 2013, authored the bestselling book *Instant Credibility Online* and written for several notable TV programs. Most importantly, I've literally written hundreds of website homepages.

In 2015 and 2016, I worked full-time at a website marketing company, writing the copy for one to five homepages per week. Since then, I've written countless homepages for other marketing agencies and via my own business. And I've devised a formula that breaks down homepage writing into a science. That process, or blueprint, as I'll soon share with you, is what you'll discover in the following pages.

Best of all?

What I'm about to teach you is incredibly simple. Simplicity is key to successful homepages, copywriting and sales in general, and this book will make homepage writing easy for you.

What you'll learn

Homepages are written in segments. If you examine many impressive homepages or check out popular ones, you'll see that. This book covers the 13 segments I most often use when writing a homepage, which include the Main Banner, Intro and Testimonials, among others. That said, this list is not exhaustive. The amount of possible segments you could create are only limited by your imagination.

This book will discuss each of the 13 segments in detail, with each chapter covering 3 core points: the purpose of each section, how to write it and when it's best to use.

There will also be plenty of visual examples. I'll provide you with links to two homepages I specifically designed for this book. Because your final homepage can be organized in countless ways, these two sample homepages, as well as my own at johnweiler.co, will give you a few ideas of how you can design yours.

To make the content of this book easy to digest, it's broken into three parts that make up the core of any homepage: Open, Middle, End.

Each part contains the different segments you can use in that area. For example, the Main Banner and Intro are covered in the Open because they establish your business's offer, value and expertise. For that reason, you should never use them in any other area on your homepage. The Middle and End also use segments that are specific to those areas and should not be used outside of them. Why?

Think of your homepage like a story. It should have an Act 1, Act 2 and Act 3, which must be told in that order, otherwise you risk confusing the visitor and causing a bounce. And this is why it's critical to keep each segment within its appropriate part.

The final part of this book will answer frequently asked questions. Like what are the most important segments, how many segments to include and the order they should go in.

The goal of this book is for you to understand how to quickly write a homepage that converts.

So shall we get down to it?

Part I

Open: Hook your visitors or risk a bounce

Your website's Open is your first impression to visitors. This is your chance to hook the reader and suck them into your website copy. Fail here, and you're certain to get a bounce.

The main point of this section is threefold. Your Open should let visitors know:

- The type of business you are (restaurant, auto repair shop, real estate agent, etc.)
- The value you offer them
- You understand their problems

Unlike the Middle and End of your homepage, there are only two segments in this part—and both I consider necessary. You'll learn why in these chapters, as well as a few key copywriting techniques to capture your visitors' attention and keep them reading. Let's get started.

1.

The Main Banner: Does your homepage pass the billboard test?

Imagine you're driving down the highway. There are dozens of billboards to your left and right. Some have big, bold images and pictures of celebrities. Others just advertise a large written message.

Now, what would happen if you saw a billboard displaying 500 words of text, all in the same font size?

Would you stop your car to read it?

Now, let's say you look to your left and see another billboard. This one has a dozen images, advertising what looks to be 10 services and 30-something words scattered about. Would you pull over and try to decipher this message?

My guess is you drove past both billboards.

You're busy. You're driving fast. You have neither the time, nor interest in some unfamiliar company's products.

Rarely is this spoken about in the website industry, but your homepage's Main Banner is a billboard for your website. With millions of distractions on the internet, attention spans are shorter than ever. And if your Main Banner doesn't get your message across quickly (as in less than five seconds) then your visitors are likely to drive past your website to their next destination.

What are the elements of an effective Main Banner?

Simplicity is key. In fact, simplicity is a key component of effective copywriting and sales in general because people can quickly understand simple messages. Make your pitch too complex or long-winded and prospects will bounce. So, will a visitor understand your message in five seconds or less?

Here are three characteristics of a simple banner:

1. Big, clearly readable message: The written message needs to be legible. Why? If people can't read it, then they'll drive past your website to another destination. In five seconds, your reader only has time to comprehend so much. That's why your readable message needs to be big, concise and contrast from its background. What do I mean by contrast?

If your message is on a light yellow background, white text will be difficult to read. It doesn't contrast well. It doesn't pop. On the opposite end of the spectrum, black text on a yellow background stands out. It's easy to read.

Readability is important because you want visitors to exert the least amount of effort possible. Understanding your business's message is a key component of the buying process. Make that buying process too difficult, and your website visitor will bounce.

2. Clean, uncluttered imagery: When there's more content for your eyes to digest, it's difficult to quickly understand a message. Less, however, is easier to see and understand. It stands out.

For example, remember the *Where's Waldo* books? Finding Waldo could easily take 10 or 20 minutes. Sure it's fun as a kid. But for adults looking to buy a new product, sifting through loads of images and text to find Waldo (aka your message) is an unwelcome chore. Most website visitors won't bother. However, a clean, uncluttered image ensures your message doesn't get lost in the crowd. It helps your visitor find Waldo fast.

3. Instant value understanding: Does your Main Banner answer the question, "What's in it for me?" Your banner is similar to an article headline. It needs to hook the website visitor immediately with value. For this reason, I always suggest that your Main Banner copy do one of two things: sell the USP (unique selling proposition) or tout benefits.

For my two websites, I use different methods for each. As you'll see below, my writer website's Main Banner is all about the benefit: Grow your business.

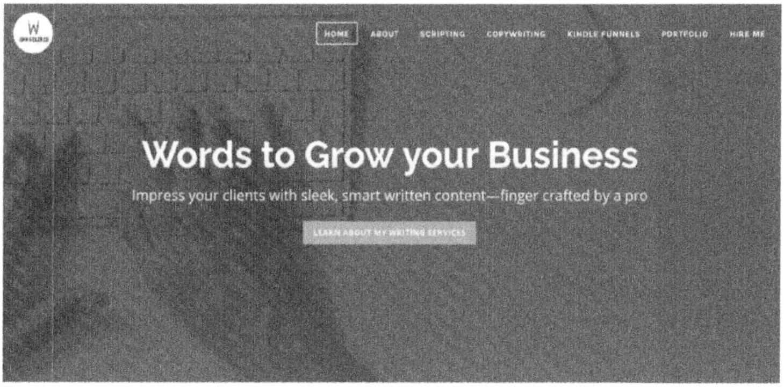

Whereas my meditation site highlights the USP: meditation for atheists, beer drinkin' dudes and religious folks.

If you have a really powerful USP, I recommend choosing that as your Main Banner copy. If experience sets you apart, like me with my writing, then you can always include that in your homepage's Intro section (directly below the Main Banner):

So, let's return to the question posed in this chapter's headline: "Does your homepage pass the billboard test?"

If you're still unsure, here are two additional questions to ask yourself:

- Can visitors understand your business's value in five seconds or less?

- Is that value strong enough to make them want to contact you or explore your website?

If you can confidently answer "yes" to those questions, then you've passed.

2.

Intro: Get ooey gooey emotional with your prospect

Emotion is an incredibly persuasive tool. Once a copywriter, salesperson or even your spouse infuses emotion into their message, there's little your brain can do to remain unaffected. Emotion influences us in business and in life. It's been used to persuade for millennia and was even noted as one of Aristotle's three pillars of persuasion.

Today, there are countless studies and books that document the power of emotions, like legendary copywriter Joe Sugarman's *The Adweek Copywriting Handbook* and a Sage Journals' study that notes how emotional messages are more easily remembered (see Endnotes for details of the study). Once you become aware of emotion's influence, you'll notice it everywhere. News anchors, article headlines and commercials all spout emotional messages to win your attention.

Why do I bring this up?

Emotion is the main ingredient in your website's Intro section. It's where you get ooey gooey emotional with your website visitor. And to do this, I recommend two techniques: empathy and what I call "Sell the Dream."

Empathy: A copywriter's best friend

Many people don't listen to each other these days. It's a sad fact. Sure we sit quietly and let the other person speak, but many of us are thinking of what we want to say or other thoughts. When this happens, the speaker doesn't feel acknowledged, doesn't feel understood. And the truth is, all of us want to feel understood. We trust people who sincerely listen to us. That's how friendships are formed, intimate relationships develop and even how sales are closed.

You almost surely know what empathy is: to understand someone else's point of view, to walk in their shoes, so to speak. From a copywriting perspective, this is important because empathy quickly builds trust. It lets the speaker know you "get them." You understand their problem and that's comforting to them. The speaker, or reader in our case, starts to trust you. Which can lead to sales.

Now, on your website, there's no speaker there to say how they're feeling. They are a quiet reader who you don't know personally, so how can we empathize with them? Well, it's not as hard as you think.

The answer depends on your industry and the solutions you provide.

To give you some examples, let me show you some screenshots from the Intros I designed specifically for this book: the ones I mentioned in the Introduction.

You're a marketing company

The first Intro is for a fictional marketing company I created called Marketing Mavericks.

See the full homepage example at: www.johnweiler.co/marketingmavericks

Notice how I describe the prospect's experience in a vivid, concrete way: silent phones, empty inboxes, another eight hours. I go on to mention the readers' emotions, empathizing with their feelings of hopelessness, frustration and struggle. Do you see how the writing shows I understand the prospects' situations? Doing this wins their trust. They think, "This company gets me. They know what I'm going through, so maybe they can help me."

Let's look at a second example.

You're a bakery

As I love all things baked goods, I couldn't resist creating my own make-believe bakery called Bakery Buddies.

Great Memories

Begin at Bakery Buddies

It's Sunday morning and you're on a mission—surprise your family with the most delicious baked goods and become hero for the day.

You stroll into the local bakery and are greeted with a "warm hello." The delightful fragrance of cinnamon and flour dance in your nostrils as you see a smorgasbord of sweets light up the glass bakery display case. You grab a dozen and hit the road. You can't wait to surprise your family.

At Bakery Buddies, we understand how our delicious baked goods, service and welcoming atmosphere positively impact your day. Whether you're bringing a box of pastries home or entertaining friends on our patio, we provide you a memorable experience that brings you more laughter, smiles and happiness.

See the full homepage example at: www.johnweiler.co/bakerybuddies

Again, notice how I get emotional with the reader, talking about the laughter, smiles and great memories the bakery creates. I do this to show I understand the readers' situations and that what they really want from a bakery is more than some donuts, but a positive experience that sparks a small boost of happiness into their day.

Sell the Dream

Now, let's talk about the second Intro technique: Sell the Dream. What's that?

We all want to live the dream, and that's what this is about—selling the ideal situation to the reader. In other words, showing them how your product solves their problem and leads to their dream outcome.

In the bakery example, the dream sold is "being the hero" for your family. When I was a kid visiting my Grandma, my Uncle Glenn used to always surprise me with some strawberry frosted donuts, becoming my hero that day. I think this is a common experience for many people and you've probably been surprised with baked goods at one point or another. I mean, who doesn't love the guy who brings donuts, bagels or muffins to the office? That person is a hero. That's the dream.

In the marketing example, the dream sold is sales, inbound leads and profits as well as turn their business around. That's what prospects really want. So give them what they want, the dream, in your Intro. See how this works?

You set up your Intro pitch showing you understand the prospects' emotions, problems and situation. Then you hit a homerun by selling them on the dream your products or services create. You emotionally highlight the problem. You sell your "dream" solution.

3 tips to empathize with your reader

To empathize with your website visitor, you need to put yourself in their shoes. To do that, describe your prospect's experience by naming some of the below in your Intro.

Thoughts: When it comes to your visitors' problems, what do they think about? What are their exact thoughts that drove them to your business? In the Marketing Mavericks Intro, this is done with the lines, "What are you doing wrong? How can you win the customers you rightly deserve?" These are probably thoughts the reader has been thinking. And by writing them out in your Intro copy, you show readers you understand them.

Emotions: How do visitors feel about their problem? Angry, frustrated, defeated? Repeat some of these emotions back in your copy. Doing this shows prospects you "get them" and understand what they're feeling. As mentioned in the Marketing Mavericks and Bakery Buddies examples, the prospects' emotions are mentioned with words like laughter, happiness, frustration, hopeless, etc.

Specific examples: Last, describe specific experiences your prospect may have had. Think about the five senses. What does your reader hear, smell, touch, see or feel when they grapple with their problem or buy your solution? In Bakery Buddies, it's the experience of walking into the bakery, hearing the "warm hello" and smelling the "delightful fragrance of cinnamon and flour." In Marketing Mavericks, the prospect sees "empty inboxes" and hears "silent phones." Creating these vivid experiences in your copy creates a strong, emotional impression that's difficult for prospects to forget.

Any other things to add in your Intro?

The above is typically how I write an Intro. That said, I'll often sprinkle in USPs or benefits if they're not mentioned in the Main Banner or I don't intend to include them elsewhere on the homepage. For this reason, I highly recommend outlining your homepage—listing the specific selling points you'll mention in each segment—before you write anything.

When to use the Intro section?

Honestly, every single homepage. I can't remember ever writing one without an Intro. Empathizing with visitors is a critical part of the sales process. It establishes trust right away and tells them they're in the right place. Don't make them guess. Show prospects you understand their problems, dreams and desires, and always include this section right under your Main Banner.

Part II

The Middle: Entice prospects with your amazing offer

So you've finished your Open. Great job. Now, in your Middle it's time to dive into your business's details and intrigue visitors with value and perhaps another splash of empathy. What benefits do you offer? What makes you special? Do you service specific industries or sell unique services? In this section, you'll answer these questions, which will help convert the right visitors into customers.

The five segments we'll cover in the Middle are:

- Services
- Industries
- Is this you?
- Benefits
- USP

You should almost never use all five segments on a single homepage, and I usually use no more than three. So that means you'll have some decisions to make about what to include. Don't worry. I'll address when and when not to use each segment, depending on your specific type of business. So ready to go? Let's start with a section that's a fan favorite of business owners.

3.

Services: Why sell only 3 services on your homepage (If any)

I know, I know, I know. You're probably excited to read this section because I said it's a business owner favorite. But I ain't gonna lie. I typically loathe writing Services sections. I get why business owners like them—they're eager to promote their services—so why am I such a hater? And perhaps more importantly, why do I include a Services section on one of my own websites? Am I just being a hypocrite?

Let's start with why I hate Services sections.

While it may sound contradictory, in most cases, a Service section does little to sell your business. Yes, it promotes your services or products. But by including it, you sacrifice valuable homepage real estate for content that neglects two critical parts of your offer: the USP and benefits.

What makes your business unique? Why buy from you? In most cases, these crucial questions aren't answered in a Services section.

The majority of Services sections are generic. They commodify your business. But really, the big problem is in the headline, which is used to emphasize the name of the service—instead of a benefit or USP. Why does this matter?

Because headlines are crucial. Their purpose is to suck the reader into your copy, and some generic service headline will rarely do that. The end result is that website visitors glaze over your Services section and valuable homepage real estate is wasted, whereas it could have sold your business, generated leads or converted sales had you written juicy headlines.

So, the big question, why on earth do I have a Services section on the Johnweiler.co homepage?!

A long time ago, when I first entered the website game, my mentor Carol Tice taught me something I'll never forget: when the benefit is obvious, consider including a Services section.

Point being, the majority of business owners know the benefit of freelance writers—they save time, help generate traffic, increase online leads and reduce their tax bill.

Instead, I focus on what makes me unique. And in this case it actually is my services. In other words, my services act as my USP. Not all freelance writers are expert copywriters or script writers. And since I invented the service Kindle Funnels, which is essentially a marketing system that captures weekly leads, my services highlight my USP by default—giving website visitors a reason to choose me.

So for you, if your services don't naturally showcase your USP, then I recommend using a more valuable section instead, like Benefits, "Is this you?" or USP. We'll cover these later in the book.

How to write a Services section

Okay, you realize that your business's benefits are obvious and services unique, so how do you write this section?

Lucky for you, it's incredibly easy.

Step 1: Use a headline and subhead to name the section's benefits or USP, like I've done below.

Content that Sells

Services to help increase your profits

Step 2: Under this, list the name of each service as a subhead.

Scripting	Copywriting	Kindle Funnels

Step 3: Finally write a short description touting the benefits or USP of each service.

Need help fleshing out your explainer video? Unsure how to get your message across and sell your product? I'll script you a video that connects with your audience and creates loyal customers who keep coming back for more. Learn More

By speaking directly to your customers' needs and desires, I'll persuade them to open their wallets. With my experience as a full-time copywriter for multiple marketing agencies, I've helped hundreds of clients do just that. Learn More

Want a steady flow of leads? Would you like to be seen as an authority in your industry? As a 4x bestselling author, I know having a book is an excellent way to gain both. As a bonus, you'll earn a nice passive income from book royalties in the process. Learn More

How many services should you list?

If you have a dozen services, should you try to include as many as possible? You probably noticed I only have three services on my homepage. Do I offer more? Yes, I also offer blogging, email marketing, brochures and most writing services you can imagine. But those don't make me special. What makes me special are the three I highlight.

Also, the more services you list in this section, the less chance your website visitors will register them.

Don't believe me?

Take this real life example from legendary copywriter Joe Sugarman.

Offering too many choices (or services) lowers conversion rates

In Joe Sugarman's book *The Adweek Copywriting Handbook*, he tells the story of his marketing campaign for the Swiss Army Watch.

Sugarman's client wanted to showcase nine different styles of watches in a single ad. The idea was that advertising all nine watches would reach the broadest market, providing a choice for every customer.

But Sugarman insisted his client run just one watch in the ad: the black colored style.

The two parties disagreed. The client logically argued that more choices equals more sales. Sugarman compromised and suggested they run a split test. Two versions of the same ad were published, one advertising nine watches and the other just one. The result?

Sugarman's ad outsold his clients three to one. In other words, for every one watch the client's ad sold, Sugarman's sold three.

Why did this happen?

The human brain is only capable of processing so much information at once. We have short attention spans. We're constantly bombarded with ads. Our brains' are naturally inclined to work as little as possible. It's not hard to see how too many choices is just more noise. A simple ad, however, is like a lighthouse in a pitchblack night. It stands out.

This is a core reason why you'll notice that my most popular book covers have only a single, simple image.

The simplicity breaks through the noise.

So back to the reason why you should offer fewer services on your homepage (and even your website in general). Simply put, the more services you list, the more bandwidth and thinking required to process all the information—and the greater chance your prospect will scroll past them. If there are only a few services listed, it's easy for the visitor to quickly understand your offer.

Moral of the story: make it easy on your visitor.

I recommend highlighting only three services on your homepage. If you must add more, list the rest elsewhere on your website.

4.

Industry: Should you highlight industries you serve?

Confession time. I rarely use an Industry section. In fact, for me this is the least used section in the entire book. **But hold up**. Before you jump to the next chapter, these sections do have benefits. I'll explain what those are and the reasons I often skip adding industries. But first, what is an Industry section anyway?

As you can see from the example above, this section highlights the industries you cater to, typically with an icon or an image that depicts the sector. Along with the image is some sales copy that describes the industry specific benefits of your product or service.

If you go with this section, I recommend listing somewhere between two and six industries on your homepage. Less than two, and there's no reason to mention you serve multiple industries (since you only serve one). And more than six, your visitors are more likely to experience the same phenomenon mentioned last chapter in the Sugarman example: they get overwhelmed with information overload, and either become confused or bounce. Neither of which is good for business.

Why an Industry section can be awesome. And why they can suck.

Industry sections can be beneficial because they let website visitors immediately know if you can help them. For example, if your visitor is an IT professional and he sees you cater to his industry, you just moved one step closer to a sale. On the other hand, if the visitor doesn't see his industry listed in this section and then bounces, that's also good news because you won't waste time selling a prospect something not offered.

At the end of the day, an Industry section helps prospects understand quickly whether or not you can help them—and that can win you the ideal client. So why am I so down on them?

Simple. "Do you specialize in my industry" isn't a question most prospects ask right off the bat. Don't get me wrong, they ask this question. But usually it's later in the sales process and, usually, even if you don't specifically cater to their industry, you've probably built enough trust at that point to close the sale anyway.

Do you need an Industry section? Ask yourself these 2 questions:

1. **How industry specific are your products and services?** If a focal point of your company is that you service specific industries and have the best solutions for clients in those industries, then by all means add this section to your homepage. Basically, if your industry-specific solutions are your business's USP, then consider the section. If not, it's probably best to skip it and save your valuable homepage real estate for another segment mentioned in this book.

2. **How big is your company?** When it comes to including an Industry section, size usually matters. The smaller your company, the less likely you should bother with an Industry section, even if you can answer "yes" to the above question. When you're small, you're still growing, still learning about your business. You may discover you can serve a wider variety of sectors than you imagined. But what if that logic doesn't apply to you? What if you're small and industry-specific services are the heart of your business? Well, I have a better solution called "Is this you?" which we'll discuss in more detail next chapter.

5.

Is this you?: Why it's usually more persuasive than an Industry section

So you're a small business who really wants to use an Industry section. But I just told you not to. What gives? Well, in this chapter I'll explain an alternative: "Is this you?"

Let's say your company specializes in marketing services for retailers, restaurants and bed and breakfasts. Sure, you could list these in an Industry style section. Or, you could speak to the prospect directly, describing who they are and their individual problems. This is where an "Is this you?" section comes in. Let me show you what it looks like:

While an Industry section simply names the type of client or industry you service, the "Is this you?" section goes deeper.

As mentioned in the Intro Chapter, empathy sells. When prospects, or anyone for that matter, actually feel listened to, when they feel someone really understands them and their problems, they open up to that person, company or whomever. Consequently, they're more likely to open up their wallet, too.

And that's exactly what an "Is this you?" section does. It shows the website visitor that you understand their problems and their specific situation.

Whereas an Industry section speaks broadly, not addressing anyone specific, an "Is this you?" section shares a personal message, tailored to a unique individual. It describes a specific problem the visitor needs help with. And that compels them to click the contact button, shoot you an email or pick up the phone and call.

How to write this section

As you may have guessed, the key to writing this section is to identify common problems your customers encounter. So ask yourself, "Which problems do I constantly solve for clients? What patterns do I notice? Do I have a client 'type' I serve again and again?"

Brainstorm these common problems as well as solutions your business offers, and name them in the headline.

In the visual example above, notice how the benefit or the problem is listed in each headline:

- Sparks growth
- Overwhelmed by digital marketing
- Don't have time
- Survival depends
- Inbound leads

When you write an "Is this you?" section, do the same: identify your prospects' problems or the benefits they want. If you can add some emotion into the mix—overwhelm, confusion, frustration, etc.—then you'll create a stronger sense of empathy that's even more likely to convert.

When and **when not** to use this section

If all your clients, regardless of industry, have the same problems, then I recommend an "Is this you?" section.

The only instance when you should avoid "Is this you?" is if you're using an Industry section. The reason? The two sections ultimately serve the same purpose, "Is this you?" just goes into more detail. Choose one or the other.

Otherwise, an "Is this you?" section can be used on any homepage where your prospects share similar problems.

6.

Benefits: The most important question in marketing

What's in it for you? No, not you, as in you reading this book. But "you" as in your customer.

The answer to this question is the guiding light to your homepage.

People are selfish by nature. I'm not saying it's a bad thing, nor is it something any of us should be ashamed of. It's just how us humans work. Even the airline industry reinforces this philosophy, rightfully so, when they tell us, "In the event of an emergency, put your oxygen mask on first." In business, relationships and life, we all want to put our oxygen mask on first.

We want to take care of our families, get that stellar promotion and be first in line at the new Disney World attraction.

Will potential customers buy from your business for unselfish reasons, like to do you a favor? Well, would you? Unless you know the business owner, you likely won't buy a product from a company out of pity or to do them a solid. And neither would your customers—so give them what they want.

Your whole homepage should scream the answer to the question: What's in it for you? This is the most important question of your homepage, website and likely even in all of marketing. Answer it or risk a bounce. In no other place should this message be louder than in your Benefits section.

How to write your Benefits section

Start by listing out the core benefits of why a visitor should do business with you. Will they save time or money? Will you provide an enchanting experience they'll remember forever?

Create a list of three to six benefits; then, you'll use these as the subheads. For example, your subheads could be as follows:

- Save time
- Save money
- Save headaches
- Earn profits while you sleep
- Enjoy a frustration-free workflow
- Impress your customers instantly

The shorter the subhead the better. Try not to go over nine words. You want your prospect to quickly absorb the benefits without getting bogged down by a ton of text.

Now, let's see what this looks like in practice with another example from Bakery Buddies:

As you can see, there are three things going on here:

1. **A standard main headline** - For all the skimmers who land on your page: "4 Reasons You'll Love Bakery Buddies."
2. **Subheads** - That highlight benefits: "Locally Owned," "Organic & Vegan Options," etc.

3. **Body copy** - Under the subheads, which further clarify "What's in it for you" and can also share your USP.

When to use the Benefits section?

The Benefits section is one of my favorites to use. It shouts from the rooftops why a visitor should contact you, sign up for your email list or buy from you. That's what we want for your homepage. So in most cases, I recommend using this section...most cases.

The exception is when you choose to use the alternative described next chapter: USP section. Besides benefits, communicating your USP is one of the most important functions of any homepage. However, you should almost always use one or the other: a Benefits section or a USP section. How do you know which is best? That just so happens to be the subject of the next chapter.

7.

USP: Should your homepage feature a Benefits or USP section?

So you're ready to shout out your value. You want to tap dance in the rain, singing a little ditty about why website visitors should buy from you. Awesome. A Benefits or USP section can help you with that, and they're one of the most important sections of your homepage for that very reason.

Simply put, visitors won't buy if they don't know your value. So now to address that tiny, little question in the last chapter. Should you use a USP or Benefits section?

Before we answer that, there's another question to address first.

What is a USP section?

As mentioned briefly in Chapter 1, USP stands for unique selling proposition. In other words, what makes you special? Why should a prospect buy from you over competitors? How is your product or service different? The answer to these questions is your USP.

What does a USP section look like? Here's an example from my business Ordinary Dude Meditation:

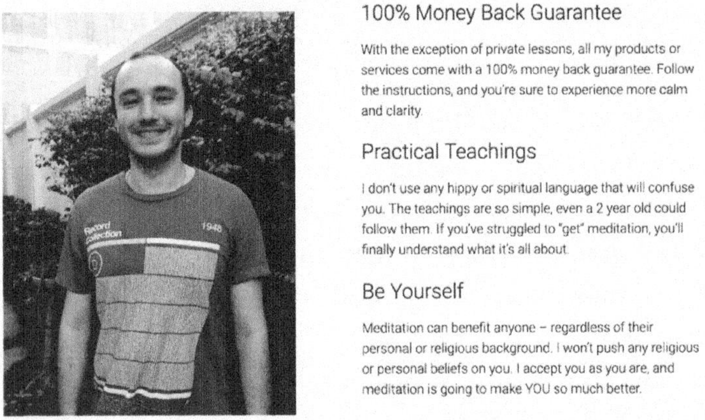

As you can see, it looks quite similar to a Benefits section. I highlight three aspects of my business that make me unique: 100% money back guarantee, practical teachings and I encourage you to be yourself. But wait a second, how do these selling points distinguish me from competitors?

Well, this whole business is designed to appeal to a different demographic of meditators. The ones who have an interest in meditation, but maybe they're atheist, cigarette smokers or blue-collar workers. These folks make up a portion of my audience. So I speak to them by indirectly saying, "Hey, you can be yourself. Just because you meditate doesn't mean you have to be religious or a hippie. You can be you."

How to write a USP section

Well, just like the above example, focus on what makes you special, what distinguishes you from your competitors.

Now there are two ways you can write a USP section. One is like my example where I highlight three unique aspects of my business. If you go this route, ask yourself, "What are my USPs?" Write them down and then break them into separate points with subheads, proclaiming the core value, just like I did in the above example and last chapter in the Benefits section. Then write a quick blurb underneath the subhead sharing more about the value you provide.

How do you write this section if you only have one USP? Well, that's the other way to go about this. I actually write one USP sections quite often for my clients. But I don't call this section a USP anymore; I call it a Resell section, which I've dedicated Chapter 12 to near the end of this book. More on this then.

Is a USP better than a Benefits section?

The simple answer is yes—a USP section is better than a Benefits section. "Then why ever write a Benefits section if I can write a USP section?" Well, a lot of times the USP is already clearly stated in the main banner or the Intro section. You don't need to waste valuable homepage real estate talking about it twice.

If you choose to write a USP section, I recommend you have multiple USPs you haven't highlighted anywhere else on the homepage. However, if you've briefly mentioned one of your USPs and feel it's important to elaborate on it, then by all means add that point to the section.

For example, I do this with my Practical Teachings feature for Ordinary Dude Meditation. The practical side of the teachings is actually already mentioned twice above my homepage's USP area. That said, this is a strong selling point of my business and could use further clarification to explain why it's important and how it helps the customer. So I include it in the USP section for this reason.

Point being, if you have multiple USPs that would benefit from a clearer description of their value or a more detailed answer to the question "What's in it for you?," then definitely include them and point them out in your USP section.

A Benefits or USP section: Why include only one or the other?

In the previous chapter, I mentioned to only use a Benefits **or** a USP section—not both. Why? Well, it's a bit overkill to use both. Doing so is like having two servings of an incredibly rich desert, like a creme brulee. For most people, it's too much. And perhaps more importantly, most businesses will just be repeating themselves if they include a Benefits and USP section, as many of these selling points will be covered thoroughly enough in just one section. That said, there've been a few instances where I have included both on a Home or Landing page. So what are these exceptions?

Well, sometimes you can handle two rich desserts if you spread them out a bit, if you have several other foods in between them. How does that translate to a homepage? If you have an incredibly long homepage, like seven or eight sections and a couple thousand words, then yes, in that case, you may want to consider adding both sections. Again, you need to make sure you're not repeating yourself. Otherwise your website visitors eyes will glaze over and you risk a bounce.

Part III

End: Close the deal

Your Open is complete. Middle is finished. Now it's time to end your homepage with a bang. This section gives your website visitor that final push to action—whether you want them to contact you, subscribe to your email list or buy a product.

Like the Middle, not all of these segments are necessary, so I'll give you some pointers on when to use them.

The segments we'll cover are:

- Blog
- Partners
- Testimonials
- Charity
- Resell
- CTA

Many of these sections are designed to prove credibility. But some also make a final sales push. Let's get into the details.

8.

Blog: When is a blog section a good idea?

Featuring your blog on your homepage isn't always a smart idea. If done under the wrong conditions, a blog can kill your business's credibility instantly. However, if inserted in the right circumstances, it can foster customer loyalty, prove authority and lead to many, many sales. How do you know whether to feature your blog on your homepage? What are the right and wrong conditions? Let's take a look.

Active blog: Do you post a minimum of twice a month? How long have you had a blog? An inactive blog on your homepage makes your website look bad, can lead to a higher bounce rate and is frankly a waste of space when it could be used for other valuable sections in this book.

The truth is blogging is hard. It's a long game that requires a continuous effort over many months and years to succeed. So if you are launching a new website, I recommend skipping a blog section. The only reason to add one is if you've been consistently blogging for six months at least twice a month. Because if you can blog consistently for that long, you're likely going to stick with it. But that isn't the only qualifying factor.

Content quality: A crappy blog hurts your credibility and shouldn't be posted on your site—homepage or elsewhere. But how do you know if your blog sucks?

Well, if you paid a non-native English speaker $15 on Fiverr to write your posts, then that's your first clue. But seriously, just ask yourself these questions: Are your blogs free of most grammar errors and run-on sentences? Does the content continually offer value? Do the headlines offer a benefit and a specific reason why a visitor should read your blog? If you can't answer an emphatic "yes" to these questions, then you probably shouldn't broadcast your blog on your homepage. And you probably shouldn't have a blog altogether.

So let's quickly recap the minimum recommended requirements to post a blog on your homepage:

- New blogs are posted at least twice a month
- Your blog has existed a minimum of six months
- Minimal grammar errors and writing faux pas, like run-on or awkward sentences
- The content offers value
- Headlines communicate a specific benefit and reason to read the blog

Assuming you can check off all those bullets, let's take a look at what a blog section looks like.

Like many of the sections in this book, you can see it looks pretty similar: there's a headline at the top, followed by the content with images. I recommend posting three to four of your latest blogs in this section.

If you have a blog, is it necessary to include a Blog section on your homepage?

It's never necessary, but whether or not you should usually depends on the content quality. While I briefly talk about this above, in my book *Instant Credibility Online* I break down blog quality further, into three tiers:

1. Low tier: Poorly written blog with generic content
2. Mid tier: Blog with repurposed, obvious content

3. Top tier: Unique and emphatic content

If your blog falls into number one, get it off your site asap. If your blog is super high quality, like tier three, then I highly recommend posting it on your homepage. Doing so will add more credibility to your business, which can increase sales. That said, don't fool yourself. The majority of blogs online fall into category number two. These types of blogs basically respin content on other websites and offer little to anything new to say. Now, you may think this is a bad thing. But not necessarily.

The word obvious is relative. What may be yesterday's news to one reader may be a new discovery for the next. It all comes down to your customer. Are they completely new to your product, service or industry? Are they beginners? If so, then what may seem obvious to you and experts, is insightful for them.

In this scenario, you may want to post your blog on your homepage. But first, consider if another section may offer more value. For example, if you have an exceptional Main Banner, Intro, Benefits, Charities and Testimonials sections, but a level two blog, I'd skip adding it. If this sounds confusing, don't worry. I'll get into more detail about choosing your homepage sections in the FAQ Chapter at the end of this book.

Before we move on, there's one last thing. If your customers are experts or have a sophisticated knowledge of your industry, you should probably avoid tier two content. Don't post it on your homepage and likely avoid it on your site altogether. If you want a blog, go for level three as it will show you speak your customers' language and are the expert they need.

9.

Partners: An easy way to quickly win trust

If you've read *Instant Credibility Online*, you'll notice a bit of overlap in this and the next two chapters: Testimonials and Charities. All three are important from a credibility perspective. However, in this book, we're going to examine these sections from a purely homepage standpoint, though credibility is a big part of that. So shall we get started? Let's talk partners.

The Logo Effect and your credibility

Also known as an Affiliations section, your Partners section wins trust through logos. I call this psychological technique the Logo Effect, which builds your credibility in two ways.

First, is via a warm connection. I introduced this concept in *Instant Credibility Online*, and am including it here again:

What is a warm connection?

What happens when you discover you share something in common with a new acquaintance? Or even better, what happens when you discover you share several interests?

You probably get excited. I know I immediately take to people who love NBA basketball. If you can talk hoops with me, I'll have a hard time ever disliking you. I'm guessing you also have a few interests that excite you as well—interests that instantly create a special bond between you and a stranger.

This is what a warm connection is. It's the things you share in common with a stranger or new acquaintance.

Warm connections are incredibly important when building trust online. In your prospects' eyes, they have the power to transform your unfamiliar business into a company run by relatable people who they could potentially become friends with. Warm connections are the first rung of trust that builds a bond between you and potential customers.

When a prospect sees a familiar logo on your website, you essentially create a warm connection.

For example, if a visitor recognizes her local chamber of commerce's logo on your site, she may suddenly think, "Hey, I attend that chamber. That's great they're partners; this company must be trustworthy if their logo is on the website."

Essentially, you gain what I call Credibility by Association. Partner logos seem like stamps of approval or endorsements from those companies—even if they're not. The more recognizable the logo, the more trust is transferred. For instance, everyone knows Google. So if you're a Google Partner, displaying their logo gives you an enormous credibility boost.

Should you add an unrecognizable logo from a small company? Yes, as long as it's impressive-looking, this is the second way a logo can improve credibility. The fact is, a logo reflects the quality of a brand. And a handful of sleek, sexy-looking logos on your website show you've partnered with quality companies. So you must be a quality company yourself, right? Again, Credibility by Association. Basically, people see a logo as a mini, unspoken testimonial for your business. So add them whenever you can.

How to create a Partners section

This section is incredibly easy to create.

All you do is write a large headline, followed by a subhead and then insert your logos.

The copy for these sections can be very simple. While I use "We're not a **household name**, but our partners are" in the above example, I could have easily gone with:

Partners you can trust
To provide service you can count on

Recognized for our quality
By these industry heavyweights

Trusted by Google
And these industry partners

With the copy written, simply add the logos underneath. But wait, where do you get the logo images, the jpeg or png files to post on your site?

Well, I'm not a lawyer, so this is not legal advice. But I'll tell you what I do. I simply Google the logo, click on the images tab at the top of search and then download the png or jpg file. If I can't find a decent image, I'll screengrab the logo and then upload it to my site. Do I ask for permission from the company who featured me?

No, and I know many other website owners who don't. The reason is it would be a time-consuming process, and if a company ever asked me to remove their logo, I'd do so in heartbeat. I doubt that'd happen, however, because I'm essentially giving them free publicity.

You can ask for permission or consult a lawyer if that makes you feel comfortable. But at the end of the day, whether or not you display another company's logo is a decision you must make on your own.

When to include a Partners section on your homepage

If you have three or more partners, then I almost always recommend including a Partners section. The only reason not too is if you have more legitimate, recognizable logos to fill a Charity section. More on that soon.

10.

Testimonials: Social proof 101

You're surely familiar with testimonials. In fact, you've probably read many when considering a product—that's because they're incredibly effective. According to the ecommerce powerhouse BigCommerce, they produce some impressive results:

- 72% of consumers report that testimonials increases their trust in a company
- 88% of buyers believe a testimonial is just as trustworthy as a recommendation from family or friends
- Shoppers who read testimonials are 58% more likely to make a purchase

What you may not know is that testimonials are a form of social proof.

What is social proof?

Social proof is public evidence that your product or service is legitimate. In other words, social proof occurs when people or companies outside your business vouch for what you're selling. Examples include endorsements or certifications from partners and affiliates, the size of your social media following and your number of article shares.

For instance, a million Likes of your Facebook page is like a million people saying, "Hey, I approve of this company." Each Like is similar to a mini-testimonial and public declaration that your business is good. Social proof, essentially. The same goes for partner endorsements and social shares. They show that society approves of your product or service.

But testimonials also affect prospects on a primal level, influencing a very old part of the human brain that's been active since our caveman days.

Testimonials and the psychology of storytelling

Storytelling is a hot topic these days. It's sexy. Marketing companies love to rave about their storytelling skills. And there's a good reason. Stories sell.

They do so because, just like visuals, they're more easily remembered than words: a well-told story creates a visual in your mind, a mental movie that's practically unforgettable. This is why our ancestors often told their tribes stories to help them remember critical lessons about safe foods to eat, trails to take and even personal history.

An effective storytelling technique most people have never heard of is called mirror characters. What's that?

Mirror characters are a key ingredient in testimonials. They reveal a potential future that can happen if the story's hero continues down a path. To illustrate this point, allow me to share three examples:

1. *Lord of the Rings* - Gollum is a mirror character for Frodo. He reflects who Frodo could become if he's seduced by the power of the ring and decides to take it as his own.
2. *Star Wars* - If Luke gives into the Dark Side, he may become just like Darth Vader. Darth Vader is his reflection. He shows a potential future for Luke, and we see this even more clearly in *Empire Strikes Back* when Luke gets a robotic hand, becoming less human and more like his father.
3. *Titanic* - Jack is a mirror character to Rose. Her life is stuck in this restrictive upper class society where she can't be herself. Jack is the opposite. He's a free spirit that takes life by the horns and lives every day to the fullest. This is why Rose falls for Jack. He reflects the deepest part of herself that yearns to be free and full of life.

So what do these examples have to do with testimonials?

The person giving the testimonial is the mirror character. They show a potential future for your prospects if they buy your product or service. In other words, prospects see themselves (or at least what they wish to see) in your testimonials. They wish to get the same result as your reviewer. This is why testimonials are so powerful.

3 aspects of credible testimonials

In *Instant Credibility Online*, I cover a simple, 2-step process to easily get testimonials and the characteristics of a credible testimonial. The latter part deserves a mention again here. Not all testimonials are created equal. In fact, if you showcase testimonials the wrong way, their effectiveness will be either minimal or non-existent. So what details do you need to create a gangbusters testimonial?

Let's revisit an excerpt from *Instant Credibility Online*:

1. Name and company

You may think one or the other is good enough, but the aim of a testimonial is not just "good enough." The purpose is to squeeze every ounce of credibility out of it so you tip a prospect's buying decision towards a sale.

A company listed without a name can come off confusing and unmemorable. And a name without a company is, well, just a name. To a prospect, there's no difference between a testimonial from a Jake Bitenhall or a Samantha Leeyon. They're both names visitors have likely never heard of. Adding the company makes the person more real and (remember this from earlier) can create Credibility by Association, or a warm connection.

2. Position

When you add an endorser's position to your testimonial, it suddenly becomes even more real. Not only does Jake Bitenhall work at Potato and Hotsauce Inc., but he's also the CEO. Wow, the C.E.O. That is impressive. Which brings up another important point. If you can get testimonials from the most important people in a company—the CEO, Managing Director or any kind of Director—then all the better. People in important positions add an extra layer of credibility.

3. Picture

An image brings the whole testimonial together, making it as real as humanly possible. The headshot is like getting that person's certified stamp of approval. If endorsers show their face and share their company info, position and name, they're putting their reputation on the line by recommending you. They're backing up their words with all their personal details. You see, testimonials create unspoken accountability. If you let down the customer, the endorser does, too. And neither of you want that, right?

People want to deal with real businesses that offer real solutions. A testimonial featuring all the above criteria helps prove that you're one of these real companies.

Once you have the above three elements, simply add them to your site along with a headline and subhead, like below:

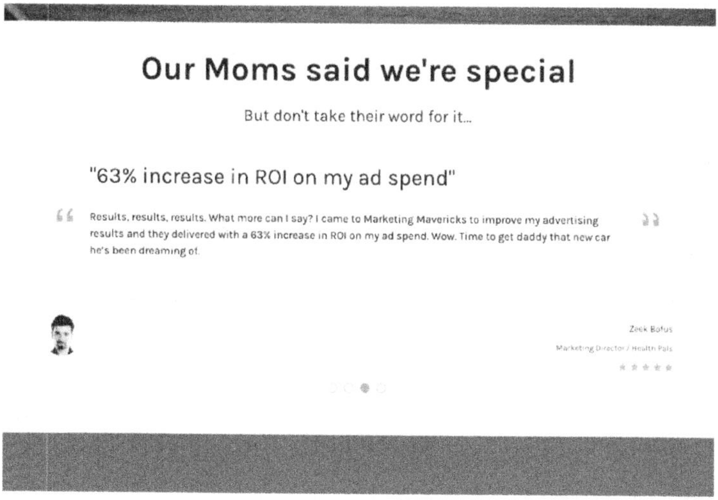

Where to put testimonials on your homepage

Now that you understand the characteristics of a credible testimonial, where should they go? I typically add them to the very bottom of a homepage, right before the CTA. Think of it like a final push to get visitors to contact you, buy your product or take whatever action you'd like.

That said, this is not the only place you can add testimonials. If you have a very long Home or Landing page, you can pepper them throughout the entire page.

How many testimonials should you get?

The more the better. I recommend aiming for at least three to start, and then build on that. If you end up getting dozens, you can even create a dedicated testimonials page to put on your site, which is basically just a page listing all of your testimonials.

When to use them?

If you have testimonials, I always recommend finding a way to squeeze them into your homepage, even if they make it longer. Their power to move visitors to action, and the fact that they're fairly easy to read because of their concise nature, are worth any extra length they may add to your page.

11.

Charity: Create a warm connection and show your goodwill

A Charity section uses two persuasion techniques to quickly build trust. Before we cover these, let me show you what this segment looks like.

As you can see, a Charity section looks similar to a Partners section, and it's essentially written in the same way. You include a headline, subhead and then logos under. Also like a Partners section, it applies some of the same persuasion tactics.

2 ways a Charity section improves conversions

The first way it persuades is through means discussed in the Partners Chapter: the Logo Effect and warm connections. I won't discuss those again here. But if you need a refresher just flip back to Chapter 9.

The second way a Charity section builds trust is rather obvious—people like supporting good-hearted companies. And when you publicize your charitable contributions, your actions show you care about more than just profits. You demonstrate your goodwill. This, along with the Logo Effect, builds trust instantly. And that leads to more conversions.

Should you use a Partners and Charity section on your homepage?

Do you remember the question about including both a Benefits and USP section from Chapter 7? Well, my recommendation for Partners and Charity sections is similar. I rarely use both on a homepage because it's a bit overkill. When creating your homepage, design and appearance must be considered. And as these two sections look incredibly similar, the design will look redundant if you include both. In other words, visitors will be more inclined to glaze over the second appearance of a Partners or Charity section because it no longer stands out. The exception?

Just like the Benefits and USP scenario, if you have an incredibly long homepage (think seven plus sections), then you may want to add both. Just space them out and insert a few other sections in between them, like a Blog, Resell, USP, etc.

If you must decide between a Partners and Charity section, choose the one with the most logos your target market will recognize. As for the section you don't use, you have a couple options:

1. Don't add it at all
2. Include the section on your About page
3. Create a dedicated page to display the extra logos and toot your own horn about why your relationships with these organizations matter. Note: this choice is probably only worth considering if you collaborate with many partners or charities.

12.

Resell: What to do when you have more to say?

So your homepage is nearly complete, but there's one tiny problem—you still have more to say, more benefits to highlight and you couldn't squeeze in a few key selling points. What should you do?

Mention anything you missed in one of the final sections of your homepage: the Resell section.

What a Resell section is

A Resell section is pretty much what it sounds like: you sell again. The selling points featured can be a combo of benefits or USPs, or a single one so special it deserves a section of its own.

Here are some examples of points I've highlighted in my clients' Resell sections:

- Prestigious awards
- 100% money back guarantees

- The client's most important industry served
- Notable stats or business results achieved for customers

To see what this looks like in practice, check out the image below:

Really, there's no hard and fast rule about what you mention here. Just include a combo of selling points you missed, or feature one outstanding selling point, achievement or USP.

Only include a Resell section when you have something to say

Remember, your website visitors' time is valuable. Only write copy that reveals your value. If you've highlighted something once, no need to say it again. For this reason, I typically include a Resell section for only 25% of the homepages I write—it's simply not needed the other 75% of the time.

The job of a copywriter is to ruthlessly edit out content, so that the final homepage, sales letter, landing page, etc. glows. Not every single selling point deserves to be highlighted on your homepage, but the truly special ones do. And when there happen to be many of those, that's when a Resell becomes your go to section.

13.

Close: Why CTAs are crucial and how to craft yours

You've done it. You've made it to the end of your homepage. Now it's time to close the deal. You need to get your visitor to take action—whether that's to subscribe to your newsletter, email you or buy something. That's where the Call to Action (CTA) comes in.

If you've never heard of the term CTA, here's a simple definition: a few words that tell your visitor what action to take next.

Below are some examples of common CTAs:

- Buy now
- Get your copy today
- Try for free
- Learn more
- Subscribe

As you can see, each CTA includes an action word that tells your website visitor what to do: buy, get, try, learn, subscribe. To provide you an even clearer idea of what this section looks like, here's an example below:

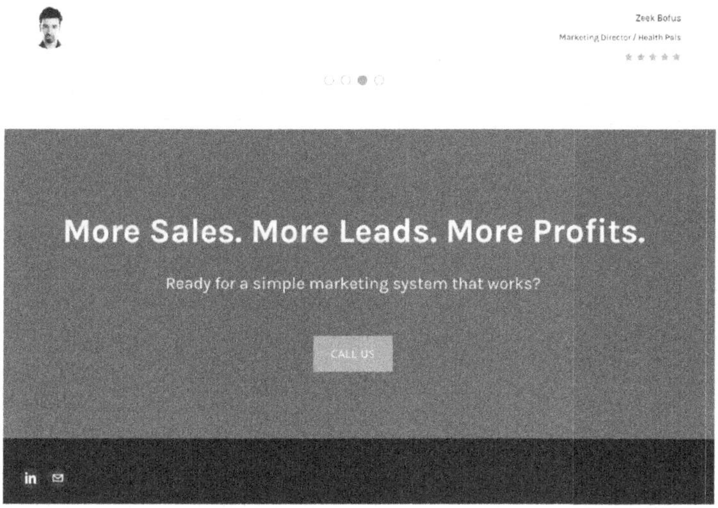

As you can see, there's a headline and subhead, like most other homepage sections in this book. Under these is the CTA that tells the visitor what to do.

Why are CTAs important?

You may think CTAs are too salesy, pointless or just unneeded. "People don't need to be told what to do," you may think.

I beg to differ. According to the UK's *Business Matters* magazine, a CTA can increase your conversion rate by 120%.

Stats aside, I've seen CTAs do wonders in my own life—homepage or otherwise. CTAs have improved my response rates in emails, landing pages and in my personal life when I ask my wife or a family member to do something.

While you may think the next step a person should take is obvious, that's usually not the case. If you don't ask or tell people the action you want them to take, there's a strong chance they'll do what most people do—nothing. Or in the case of your website, bounce.

A few ways to think of your homepage CTA

I recommend that your CTA is the last section of your homepage. And for this reason, you may want to think of it like a close, as in closing a sale. Above it, you've empathized with the visitor's problem in the Intro, pitched them the benefits and proved your credibility with the Logo Effect or testimonials. Now they're warmed up to you, it's time to push them to action.

Note that just because I'm calling this a close, doesn't necessarily mean you ask for a sale. Instead, your CTA can be for them to subscribe to your email list, contact you or simply learn more about your business or your product. Whatever you want, just tell them to take action. Close the deal.

While closing a sale is the obvious metaphor for this section, I typically think of it differently. And instead of calling it a CTA, I usually call this section a Button. What does that mean?

Well, the term is from the movie world and it means to finish a scene with a memorable visual or bit of dialogue that ends it on a high note. Sometimes the Button will evoke a laugh or smile from the audience. Either way, the word button implies the phrase "put a button on it"—as in put the finishing touches on it, which is what many screenwriters aim for in individual scenes. Why? Buttons create a little boost of interest or engagement that propels the moviegoer into the next scene.

Buttons keep a movie's pace moving forward, and they can do the same when used in your CTA section. I often used buttons when writing scripts for A&E, National Geographic and my own personal projects, and I use them all the time on homepages.

Whether you call this segment a Close or a Button, they both include a CTA. And now that your website visitors have read about your offer, pitch and the value you provide, they're primed to take action. You've built some trust with all the content from your homepage, so if they are going to act, your best chance is now.

What to say in your Close section?

Just like your main banner copy, you want your Close to tout benefits or the USP. And speaking of which, when I write main banner copy, I typically craft three to six headlines and then choose the best or most appropriate one. Sometimes, I have a couple good options left over and I'll use my next favorite or one that touches on a different USP, for the Close.

I should note that in your Close, it's okay to repeat selling points you've covered elsewhere on the homepage. The fact is, most people won't read all of your HP copy—they'll skim it. So you want to highlight a major selling point here that will really push them to action. Give them something juicy, something irresistible, and you'll see conversions increase.

When to use the Close section?

No question, use this segment on every single homepage or landing page you write. The hard truth is that a good portion of website visitors don't get past the homepage, so tell them exactly what action to take in your CTA.

FAQ

Answers to 4 common homepage questions

If you've never written a homepage before, you may feel a bit overwhelmed now. We've covered a ton of content and you likely have questions: Which segments should I include? How do I order them? How can I write my homepage in the least amount of time?

Don't worry, this FAQ will answer these nagging questions. So let's get started.

1. What are the most important sections of a homepage?

While you've learned about when and why to use the various homepage segments in this book, you may wonder which are most important. Are some sections more essential than others? The answer is yes.

So let me break it down for you into three levels of importance.

Level 1: Essentials

At a minimum, I recommend always including the four sections below:

- Main Banner
- Intro
- Benefits or USP
- Close

These sections are needed because they focus on the value you provide. No prospect will choose your business if you don't share your value—so don't miss out on potential customers.

Level 2: Nice to have, not have to have

If I had to choose the second tier of important segments, it would be as follows:

- Is this you?
- Blog
- Partners
- Testimonials
- Charity
- Resell

These six segments either show credibility, value or empathy for the customer's plight. In 99% of homepages I write, I use a combination of them. Which ones you use is up to you. Follow the advice in the specific chapter to know which section is best for your business and, as the heading above suggests, all these are optional.

Level 3: Likely skip

These sections I like about as much as a dry wedding. You can typically skip:

- Services
- Industry

As appealing as these sections are to many business owners, they typically don't offer much value for the visitor and instead commodify your business. Generally, you only want to include them if they highlight your USP. See the specific chapter to get a better understanding of why.

2. How many sections should I include?

I recommend a minimum of the essential four: Main Banner, Intro, Benefits or USP and Close.

In most cases, a shorter homepage is better because it forces you to ruthlessly cut out trivial sales points—and instead highlight your unique value. For this reason, I usually shoot for five to seven segments. If you have more, that's okay. Though I would cap it at eight or nine tops.

However many you choose, just remember, your website visitor's time (just like yours) is valuable. Avoid repeating yourself, edit out fluff mercilessly and only mention your business's most noteworthy selling points.

3. How should I order the segments?

Always start with the Main Banner. Second is always the Intro. After that, you can improvise some for the middle, which include the following potential segments:

- Industry
- Services
- Is this you?
- Benefits/USP

At a minimum, use the Benefits, USP or "Is this you?" section. You know how I feel about Industry and Services, so use those at your own discretion.

The next segments are the following:

- Blog

- Partners
- Testimonials
- Charity
- Resell

You can use one to all of these sections, though generally, less is more. I rarely use all of them myself.

The final segment of your homepage, which I always recommend including, is the Close.

One final and important tip: only half the battle of an effective homepage is the copywriting, the other half is design. So I recommend being mindful of which segments you put next to each other.

A good idea is to alternate heavy visual sections with heavy text sections. For example, the typically text-heavy Resell segment fits perfectly between the more visual Testimonials and Partners sections. On the opposite end of the spectrum, a Services segment that highlights three services, followed by a Benefits segment that highlights three benefits will generally look too similar, making the design look boring, redundant and easy for visitors to glaze over.

4. What is the quickest way to write a homepage?

It could take you anywhere from 2 hours to 20 hours, depending on how fast of a writer you are. That said, I typically knock them out in two to four hours.

To answer this question though, the quickest way to write a homepage is to use a system. As I have a ton of experience and have written hundreds of homepages, let me share mine.

Whenever I'm about to write a homepage, I first read the client's brief and then look at my list of potential segments to include:

Main Banner
Intro
Industries
Blog
Partners
Testimonials
Services
Resell
CTA
Charity
Benefits / USP / Is this you?

From there, I choose the segments I think will best sell the client's business. How do I choose? It depends on the client's USP and main benefits offered. So I search their brief for these selling points and highlight them.

Next I outline the homepage and order the sections. Then I briefly list the specific selling points I want to touch on in each segment. Note that while doing this, sometimes I find that one segment isn't working, so I'll swap it out for a more appropriate one.

Once this is complete, the writing begins. As the Main Banner is critical to hooking your visitor, I start here, writing three to six headlines as mentioned in Chapter 13. From there, I just freestyle and write the sections in whichever order I feel.

Conclusion

Links to sample homepages and a word from the author

I hope you enjoyed this book and it's helped you learn a simple formula for writing your homepage. My goal was to make the process as easy as possible, and show you exactly how a professional has done it for hundreds of websites.

That said, I appreciate your feedback. I read all reviews and have actually changed content in my previous books based on readers' comments. So don't be shy. Please let me know your thoughts in a review, and feel free to let me know if I missed anything.

Before I forget, here are the links to the sample homepages designed specifically for this book and mentioned throughout:

- Marketing Mavericks: www.johnweiler.co/marketingmavericks
- Bakery Buddies: www.johnweiler.co/bakerybuddies

I hope they prove to be helpful references for you.

If you have any questions about writing a homepage, or are looking for a copywriter to do it for you, don't be a stranger. Contact me today at john@johnweiler.co.

I look forward to helping you succeed with your website.

Cheers,
John

Also by John Weiler

Does your website make you look like an amateur or an influencer?

Every website sends subtle signals to visitors that reveal its trustworthiness. Which signals is yours sending? Learn how you can quickly prove your authority in *Instant Credibility Online: 25 tactics to win website visitors' trust. And go from nobody to influencer in 6 months or less.*

Available at Amazon.com

The bestselling *Ordinary Dude Guide* series, ordered 10,000+ times.

Special Thanks

To my editors Cheyenne Hollis and Ryan Farley. Thanks for your clear and concise edits and suggestions. Your work on this book made this the easiest final draft I've ever completed.

To my friends at Pronto Marketing and Cory and Derek Brown. Thanks for giving me a shot as a copywriter back in 2015. This book likely wouldn't be here if it weren't for you.

To my wife, Arissara Weiler, and to my parents, James and Diane Weiler. Thank you for the support as I continue to write books. I love this work and it makes me smile whenever you ask me, "How is the book business doing?"

About the author

John Weiler began his writing career in 2009 as a writer for the TV series *Three Sheets*, which aired on the Travel Channel, The Fine Living Network and Spike TV. He continued writing in TV till 2012 when he was a writer on National Geographic's hit TV series *Alaska State Troopers*.

In 2014, John transitioned into copywriting, blogging and book publishing, working for several marketing agencies along the way and publishing five bestselling books. You can learn more about his writing career and services at www.johnweiler.co.

Outside of the writing world, John is an NBA fanatic, meditator of 17 years and a beer connoisseur (if you can say that's a thing).

Get in touch with him at john@johnweiler.co.

Endnotes

Chapter 1

8 Remember the *Where's Waldo?* books. Martin Handford, *Where's Waldo?* (Somerville, MA: Candlewick Press, 2019). This citation is specifically for the original *Where's Waldo?* book; however, "finding Waldo" is something that's done in all books in the series.

Chapter 2

12 Persuade for millennia. William Harris (January 15, 2018) "What Aristotle Can Teach You About Marketing," Entrepreneur, https://www.entrepreneur.com/article/306880 (accessed May 15, 2021)

12 Legendary copywriter Joe Sugarman's. Joseph Sugarman, *The Adweek Copywriting Handbook: The Ultimate Guide to Writing Powerful Advertising and Marketing Copy from One of America's Top Copywriters* (Hoboken, New Jersey: John Wiley & Sons, Inc., 2007), Kindle.

12 A Sage Journals' study. Matthew D. Rocklage, Derek D. Rucker, Loran F. Nordgren (March 15, 2018) "Persuasion, Emotion, and Language: The Intent to Persuade Transforms Language via Emotionality," SAGE Journals, https://journals.sagepub.com/doi/abs/10.1177/0956797617744797 (accessed May 15, 2021)

Chapter 3

26 In Joe Sugarman's book. Sugarman, *The Adweek Copywriting Handbook*, 172-174

Chapter 10

58 Ecommerce powerhouse BigCommerce. Emily Cullinan. "How to Use Customer Testimonials to Generate 62% More Revenue From Every Customer, Every Visit," BigCommerce Blog, https://www.bigcommerce.com/blog/customer-testimonials/#social-media (accessed May 15, 2021)

60 Lord of the Rings. *The Lord of the Rings Trilogy*. Directed by Peter Jackson. 2001-2003. Burbank, CA: New Line Cinema, Blu-ray Disc.

60 Star Wars. *Star Wars: Episode V, The Empire Strikes Back.* Directed by Irvin Kershner. 1980. Beverly Hills, CA: Lucasfilm, Blu-ray Disc.

60 Titanic. *Titanic*. Directed by James Cameron. 1997. Hollywood, CA: Paramount Home Entertainment, Blu-ray Disc.

Chapter 13

74 According to the UK's *Business Matters*. (July 12, 2017) "How important is a Call to Action?," Business Matters, https://bmmagazine.co.uk/marketing/important-call-action/ (accessed May 15, 2021)

Made in the USA
Monee, IL
08 November 2026

68002059R00059